WRITER AND ILLUSTRATOR:
SHIRLEY WILLIS was born in Glasgow. She has worked as an illustrator, designer and editor, mainly on books for children.

READING CONSULTANT:
BETTY ROOT was the Director of the Reading and Language Information Centre at the University of Reading for over twenty years. She has worked on numerous children's books, both fiction and non-fiction.

TECHNICAL CONSULTANT:
PETER LAFFERTY is a former secondary school science teacher. Since 1985 he has been a full-time author of science and technology books for children and family audiences. He has edited and contributed to many scientific encyclopaedias and dictionaries.

EDITOR:
KAREN BARKER SMITH

Published in Great Britain in MMXIX by
Book House, an imprint of
The Salariya Book Company Ltd
25 Marlborough Place, Brighton BN1 1UB
www.salariya.com

ISBN: 978-1-904194-13-2

SCRIBO   BOOK HOUSE   SCRIBBLERS

1 3 5 7 9 8 6 4 2

A CIP catalogue record for this book is available from the British Library.

Printed and bound in Malaysia.

Visit
www.salariya.com
for our online catalogue and
free fun stuff.

PAPER FROM

SUSTAINABLE
FORESTS

WhiZ Kids

CONTENTS

Wherever you see this sign, ask an adult to help you.

WhiZ KidS
Tell me how fast it goes

Written and illustrated by
SHIRLEY WILLIS

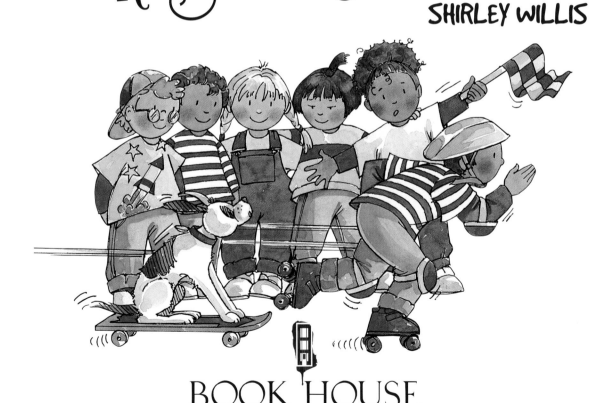

BOOK HOUSE
a SALARIYA *imprint*

HOW CAN I RUN?

Your muscles make every part of your body move. Strong muscles help you run fast.

READY!

SET!

Go!

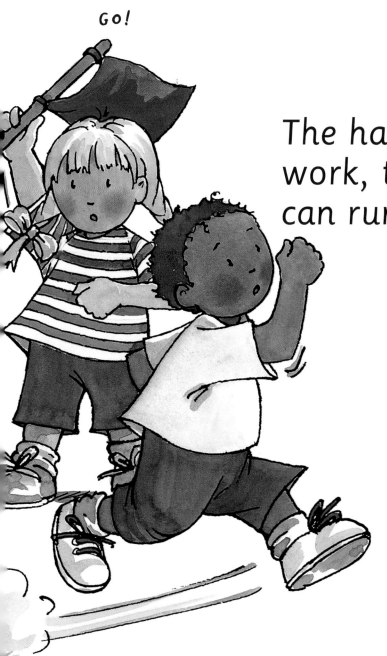

The harder your muscles work, the faster you can run.

We have muscles all over our bodies. You can feel your muscles working. Make a fist and feel the muscles at the top of your arm bulge.

HOW DO WE MEASURE SPEED?

Speed is how fast things travel.
It is measured over an exact distance, like a mile or a kilometre.

READY, SET, GO!

Measure out a set distance and take turns to run. You'll need a stopwatch to time each run to find out who is fastest.

If you can run 1 kilometre in one hour, your speed is 1 kilometre per hour.

1 KILOMETRE AN HOUR IS CALLED 1 KPH FOR SHORT!

ARE FOUR LEGS BETTER THAN TWO LEGS?

Snails are the world's slowest animals. They travel at 0.05 kph.

Many animals can run faster than we can because they have stronger muscles. Animals have powerful muscles that help them run very fast.

Cheetahs are the world's fastest animals. They can travel at 100 kph.

A CAT CAN RUN AT 48 KPH!

WHOOSH!

11

HOW CAN I GO FASTER?

Wheels make you go faster. A machine with wheels helps you to make better use of your muscles.

The harder your muscles work, the faster the wheels spin around.

I CAN'T RUN AS FAST AS THIS!

PEDAL POWER

The harder you push on the bicycle pedals, the faster the wheels spin.

Bicycles and skateboards are machines with wheels.

13

WHY DOES OUR BALL SLOW DOWN?

As the ball rubs
against the grass,
it causes friction.
This makes the ball
slow down until
it stops rolling.

Friction causes heat.
Rub your hands together
- do they feel warm?
Now try it with soapy hands
- they don't get so warm.
Slippery hands cause
less friction.

Friction is caused
when things rub
together.
Friction makes things
slow down.

WHY DO SKIS SLIDE?

Snow and ice are very smooth. Skis are smooth, too. Skis slide easily because there is not much friction.

SMOOTH SURFACES CAUSE LESS FRICTION!

Without much friction,
it can be difficult to stop.

17

HOW CAN I SWIM FASTER?

When you swim, you cause friction in the water. This slows you down. You can swim faster if you cause less friction.

You cause less friction by moving through the water as smoothly as you can.

A long, smooth body shape glides through the water quicker.

Jumping into the water makes a big splash that slows you down.

TRY NOT TO SPLASH MUCH — IT SLOWS YOU DOWN!

19

WHY DO SOME BOATS HAVE SAILS?

Boats with sails use wind power.
When wind blows into the sails,
it pushes the boat along.

The stronger the wind,
the faster the boat can go.

SAIL AWAY!

You will need:
- A plastic tub
- A plastic straw
- Modelling clay
- A piece of paper
- Sticky tape

1. Make a sail with the straw and paper (as shown).
2. Press a blob of modelling clay onto the bottom of the tub.
3. Push the straw into the clay.
4. Now blow!

WHY DO CARS GO FAST?

Cars go fast because
they have engines.
Engines are more powerful
than human or
animal muscles.

Air acts like a brake – it makes a moving car slow down. Fast cars have smooth, rounded shapes to help them move faster through the air.

Fast cars have more powerful engines than slow cars.

WHAT MAKES TRAINS GO?

Trains are pulled by powerful engines. The engine power comes from electricity. The electricity comes from overhead electric wires or from a rail by the track.

A wire frame called a pantograph carries electricity from overhead wires to the engine.

WHY DO PLANES ROAR?

Planes have powerful jet engines that make them go very fast.

THAT NOISE HURTS MY EARS!

JET ENGINE

Burning gases rush from the back of a jet engine and push the plane forward at great speed.

Jet engines are powered by burning gases.
As the gases burn, they make a loud roar.

You can use air to make a loud noise. Blow up a paper bag and hit it very hard. It will explode with a bang.

WHY DOES IT GO SO FAST?

Space rockets have the most powerful engines.
A rocket engine needs to be powerful enough to push a rocket into space.

Rocket engines are powered by burning gases. The burning gases push the rocket upwards.

TO GO INTO SPACE, A ROCKET MUST TRAVEL AT 40,000 KPH!

LIFT OFF!

Blow up a balloon
and let it go.
As the air inside
quickly escapes, it
pushes the balloon
through the air.

29

GLOSSARY

distance   The amount of space between two objects or places.

electricity   A type of power that makes many machines work. It comes from electricity power stations.

engine   A device that drives many machines.

friction   A braking action caused when two things rub together.

jet engine   An aircraft engine that pushes hot gases out of the back of a plane to push the plane forward.

kilometre   A unit of length that measures 1,000 metres.

muscles   The parts of the body in humans and animals that make all movement possible.

pantograph   A device that feeds electricity to the engine of a train from the electric wires overhead.

rocket   A powerful machine that carries spacecraft into space.

sail   A piece of cloth attached to a boat that catches the wind and pushes the boat forward.

speed   How quickly something moves.

wind power   The power of the wind that makes an object move.

INDEX